worker!

I am
brilliant!

I'm a
star!

Super
worker!

Well
done!

Adding and Taking Away

Ages 5–6

Written by Paul Broadbent

Bath · New York · Singapore · Hong Kong · Cologne · Delhi · Melbourne

Helping your child

⭐ Do talk about what's on the page. Let your child know that you are sharing the activities.

⭐ Explain what has to be done on each page, and help with any recording such as colouring and joining up. Pencil control in young children is not usually very well developed.

⭐ Do not become anxious if your child finds any of the activities too difficult. Young children develop and learn at different rates. It is quite common to find children who seem not to want to learn, and who then suddenly put on a spurt once they are ready.

⭐ Let your child do as much or as little as he or she wishes. Do leave a page that seems to be difficult and return to it later.

⭐ It does not matter if your child does some of the pages out of turn.

⭐ The answers to the activities are on page 32.

⭐ Always be encouraging, and give plenty of praise.

Illustrated by Adam Linley

This edition published by Parragon in 2009

Parragon
Queen Street House
4 Queen Street
BATH, BA1 1HE, UK

ISBN 978-1-4075-7531-5
Printed in China

Contents

Numbers to 10	4		Counting on	20
Counting	6		Counting back	22
Comparing	7		Addition bonds	24
Putting together	8		Subtraction bonds	26
How many are left?	10		Second chance	27
Finding differences	11		Addition facts	28
Number machines	12		Subtraction facts	30
Second chance	14		Answers	32
Hidden numbers	15			
Adding	16			
Taking away	18			

Numbers to 10

Trace the numbers. Join each kite to the right number. Join each number to the right group of pictures at the bottom of each page.

Note for parent: Ask your child to say each number and word aloud as he or she traces over them.

six seven eight nine ten

6 7 8 9 10

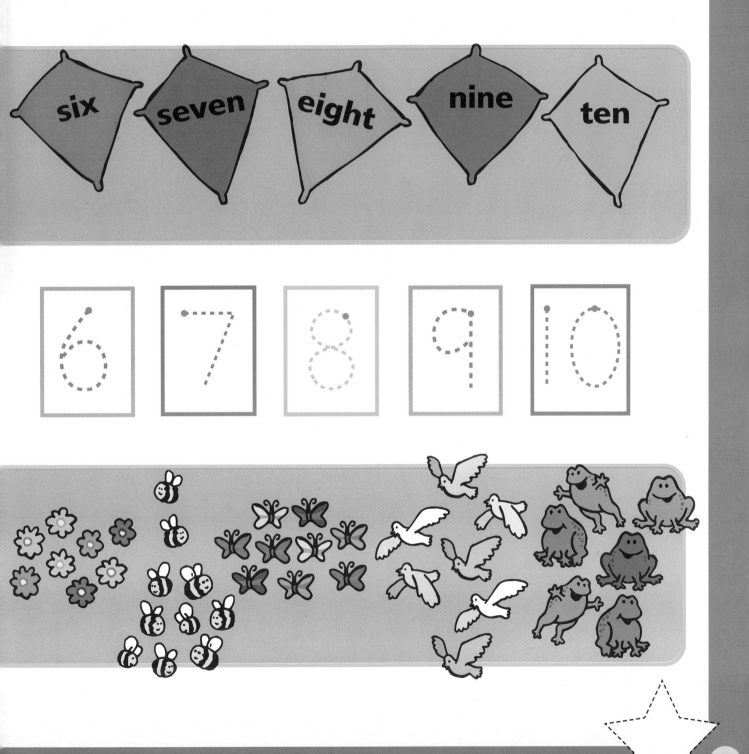

Counting

Count the objects in the big picture.
Write the correct number in each box.

Note for parent: To help find the totals, children can mark each object as they count.

Comparing

Colour most spaceships red. Colour the rest of the spaceships blue. Write the numbers in the boxes.

☐ red spaceships

☐ blue spaceships

☐ red spaceships

☐ blue spaceships

☐ red spaceships

☐ blue spaceships

☐ spaceships altogether

☐ red spaceships

☐ blue spaceships

☐ spaceships altogether

Note for parent: Your child can choose the number of spaceships to colour red, but there must be more red spaceships than blue ones.

7

Putting together

Count each set. Write how many there are altogether.

biscuits altogether

cakes altogether

pizzas altogether

ice creams altogether

sweets altogether

 Note for parent: Encourage your child to count on from the first number to find the total.

Count the spots on each monster.
How many spots are there altogether?

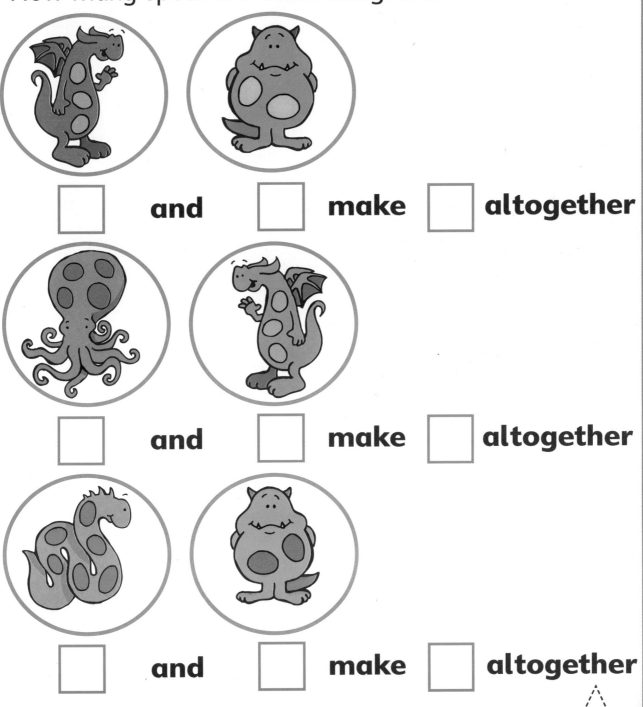

[ ] **and** [ ] **make** [ ] **altogether**

[ ] **and** [ ] **make** [ ] **altogether**

[ ] **and** [ ] **make** [ ] **altogether**

How many are left?

Cross out two in each set. Write how many are left.

5	take away	2

leaves ☐

6	take away	2

leaves ☐

8	take away	2

leaves ☐

4	take away	2

leaves ☐

Some birds are flying away.
How many are left on the branch?

9 take away 3 leaves ☐

Note for parent: This activity will help your child to recognize numbers and match them to an amount.

Finding differences

How many more children are there than chairs?

☐ children

☐ chairs

difference → ☐

☐ children

☐ chairs

difference → ☐

☐ children

☐ chairs

difference → ☐

Note for parent: Finding the difference is the same as counting on from the smaller number to the larger one.

Number machines

Sweets go into these adding machines.
Write how many come out of each machine.

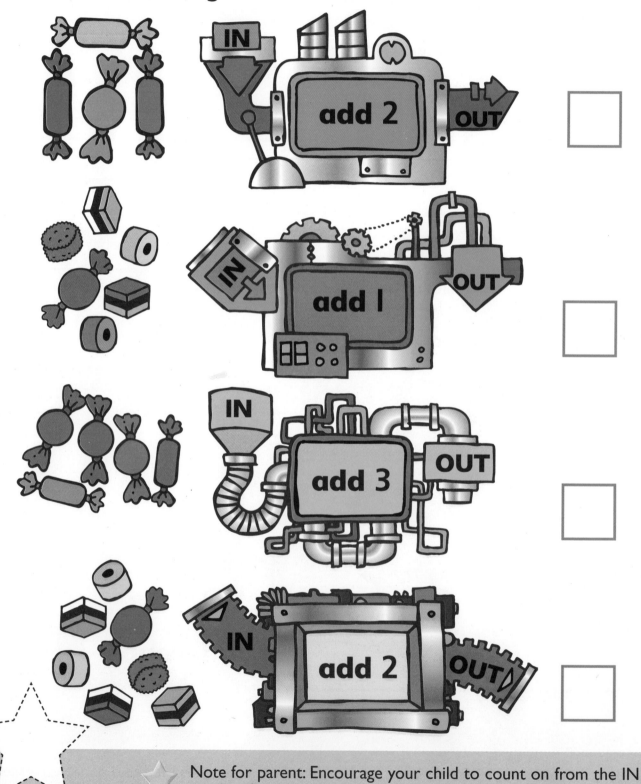

Note for parent: Encourage your child to count on from the IN number for adding, and to count back for taking away.

Drinks go into these take-away machines.
Write how many come out of each machine.

13

Second chance

Count each set. Write how many there are altogether.

☐ **biscuits altogether**

☐ **cakes altogether**

Count the spots on each monster.
How many are there altogether?

☐ **and** ☐ **make** ☐ **altogether**

Cross out two in each set. Write how many are left.

8	**take away**	**2**
leaves	☐	

4	**take away**	**2**
leaves	☐	

14

Note for parent: This page helps to find out what
your child can remember.

Hidden numbers

There are 9 rabbits in each line.
Write how many are hidden.

 Note for parent: Ask your child to count how many
rabbits, then count on to 9 to find the difference.

Adding

Draw the extra balloons in each row.
Write the correct totals.

2 add 3

$2 + 3 =$ ☐

3 add 4

$3 + 4 =$ ☐

4 add 5

$4 + 5 =$ ☐

Write how many there are altogether.

☐ **+** ☐ **=** ☐

☐ **+** ☐ **=** ☐

Note for parent: Make sure your child recognizes the addition sign (+) and the equal sign (=).

Write how many coloured pencils there are altogether.

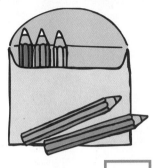

3 + 2 = ☐

2 + 2 = ☐

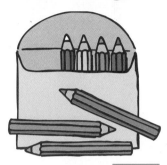

4 + 3 = ☐

5 + 1 = ☐

6 + 3 = ☐

4 + 5 = ☐

Join each sum to the correct total.

5+2   3+3   4+1   1+3   4+4

5   8   6   7   4

17

Taking away

Two children get out of each of these trains.
How many are left on each train?

7 take away 2 is ☐   **7 – 2 =** ☐

5 take away 2 is ☐   **5 – 2 =** ☐

8 take away 2 is ☐   **8 – 2 =** ☐

Cross out some flags. Write how many are left.

9 – ☐ **is** ☐

Note for parent: Make sure your child recognizes the subtraction sign (–). Remember to use the words 'subtract' and 'take away'.

Draw how many balls come out of the machines. Write the totals in the red boxes.

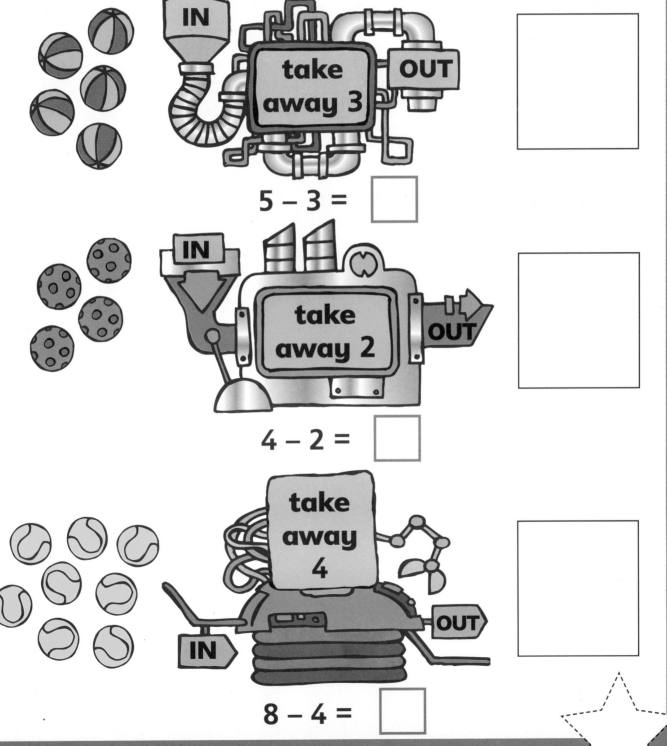

5 – 3 =

4 – 2 =

take away 4

8 – 4 =

Counting on

Use the number track to count on. Show the jumps and write the answer. The first one has been done for you.

4 + 2 = 6

5 + 3 =

7 + 2 =

3 + 4 =

6 + 4 =

2 + 3 =

Note for parent: These activities will help your child to use a number track or number line to count on to find a total.

Join each rocket to the correct answer on the number line.

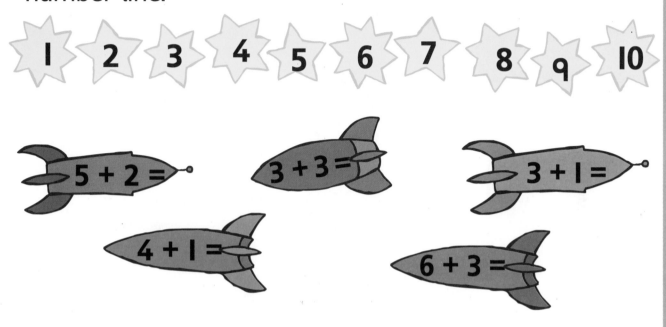

1 2 3 4 5 6 7 8 9 10

5 + 2 =

3 + 3 =

3 + 1 =

4 + 1 =

6 + 3 =

Write the missing numbers in these counting patterns.

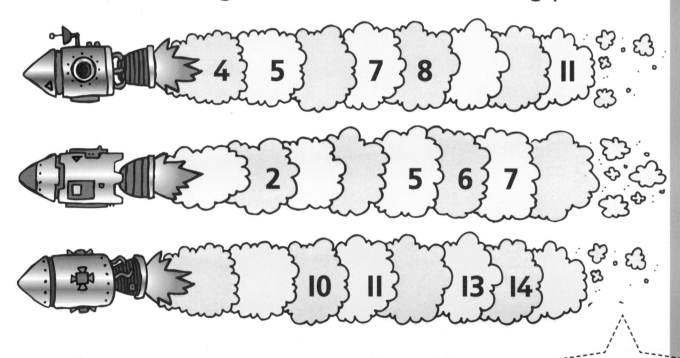

4 5 ⬡ 7 8 ⬡ ⬡ 11

⬡ 2 ⬡ ⬡ 5 6 7 ⬡

⬡ ⬡ 10 11 ⬡ 13 14 ⬡

Counting back

Use the number line to count back. Show the jumps and write the answer.

6 – 3 = ☐

5 – 2 = ☐

8 – 4 = ☐

9 – 3 = ☐

10 – 2 = ☐

7 – 6 = ☐

Note for parent: Counting back on a number line or number track is a good method for taking away.

Work out each answer. Colour the correct number in the number track to match.

Addition bonds

Make these totals in different ways.
Write the answers in the boxes.

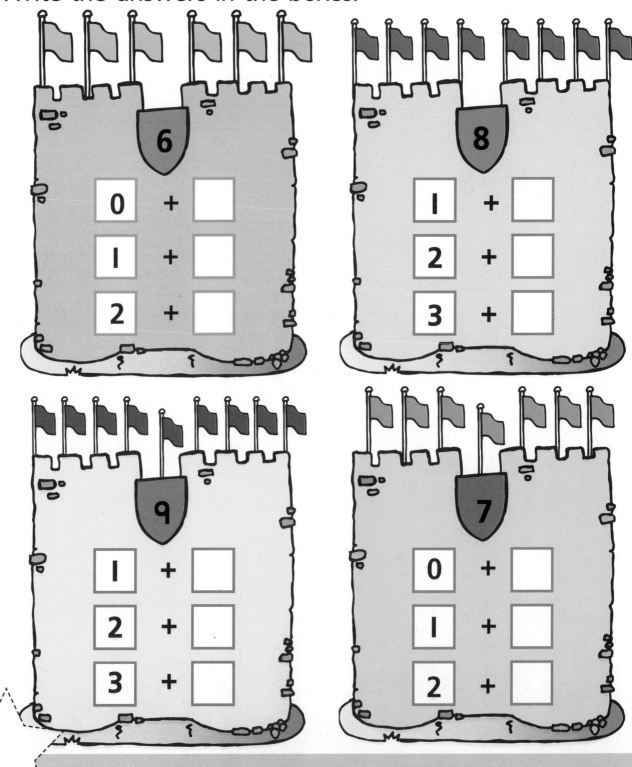

6

0	+	
1	+	
2	+	

8

1	+	
2	+	
3	+	

9

1	+	
2	+	
3	+	

7

0	+	
1	+	
2	+	

Note for parent: Addition bonds are all the different ways that a total can be made with two numbers.

Draw a line from each flower to the pot with the correct total.

6 + 3   6 + 2   8 + 2   3 + 5   5 + 4

7 + 3   4 + 6   8 + 1   4 + 4

8   9   10

What can you see if you colour all the shapes with a total of 10?

6 + 3
8 + 1   1 + 4   0 + 7
                              8 + 3
9 + 1   4 + 6
         7 + 3   7 + 1 8 + 0
5+6
     5 + 5   0 + 10 1 + 9   3 + 2
2 + 6   5+8
         8 + 2
              3 + 7
4 + 4   0 + 9   7 + 2   4 + 8

Subtraction bonds

Find different ways of making 3 and 4.

3
4 – 1
7 –
3 –
9 –
8 –

4
7 –
5 –
9 –
8 –
6 –

Find different ways to make the answer of 5.

Note for parent: These activities will help your child to learn the subtraction bonds within 10.

Second chance

Join the sums to the correct totals.

5+2   4+1   4+4

5   8   7

Draw how many balls come out of the machines.

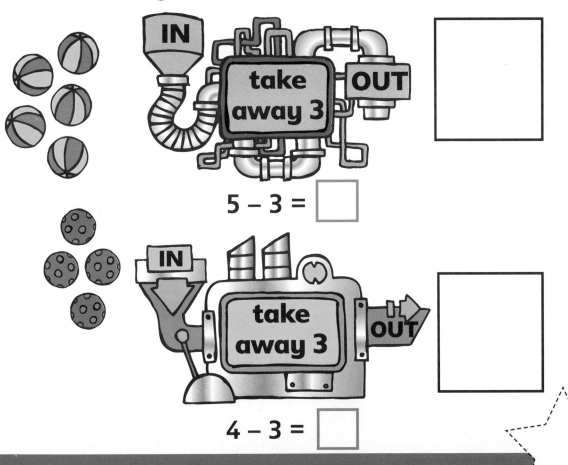

IN   take away 3   OUT

5 − 3 = ☐

IN   take away 3   OUT

4 − 3 = ☐

Note for parent: This page helps to find out what your child can remember.

Addition facts

Write the answers in the boxes. Use the number track to help you.

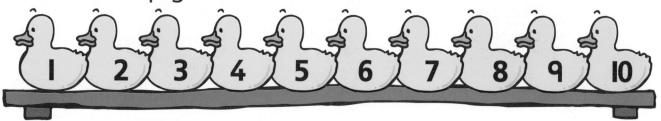

4 + 3 = ☐   6 + 2 = ☐   5 + 5 = ☐

9 + 1 = ☐   7 + 2 = ☐   3 + 5 = ☐

2 + 4 = ☐   4 + 4 = ☐   6 + 3 = ☐

The top can is the total of the two cans below. Write the missing numbers. The first one has been done for you.

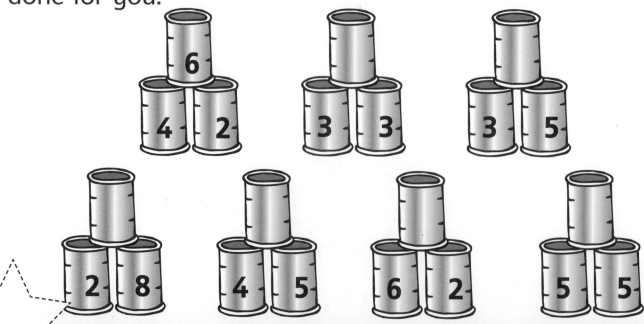

Note for parent: Talk about the different ways that totals are made.

Write the missing numbers.

+ 3 = 7

+ 2 = 5

4 + = 9

6 + = 9

+ 8 = 10

5 + = 8

+ 2 = 8

3 + = 6

+ 7 = 10

Follow these trails to reach 10.
Write the missing totals.

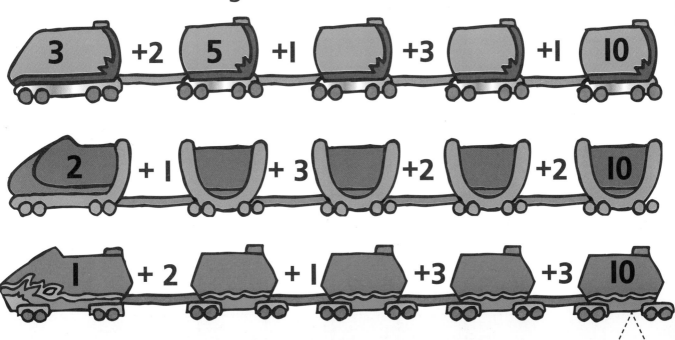

3 +2 5 +1 +3 +1 10

2 +1 +3 +2 +2 10

1 + 2 + 1 +3 +3 10

Subtraction facts

Write the answers in the boxes. Use the
number track to help you.

0 1 2 3 4 5 6 7 8 9 10

6 – 4 = ☐   7 – 3 = ☐   5 – 1 = ☐

8 – 5 = ☐   6 – 3 = ☐   9 – 4 = ☐

10 – 5 = ☐   7 – 4 = ☐   8 – 3 = ☐

Colour the squares that have an answer of 4.
What can you see?

6 – 1	5 – 1	7 – 2	7 – 4	8 – 2	8 – 3
5 – 2	7 – 3	6 – 3	10 – 1	9 – 7	5 – 4
3 – 2	10 – 6	8 – 5	4 – 4	6 – 4	10 – 5
10 – 7	4 – 0	9 – 6	9 – 5	5 – 0	6 – 5
8 – 3	8 – 4	6 – 2	5 – 1	7 – 3	4 – 4
5 – 3	9 – 4	7 – 1	10 – 6	8 – 6	3 – 0

Note for parent: These activities give practice in
learning the subtraction facts within 10.

Write the missing numbers.

⬡ – 4 = 3   △ – 2 = 4   ⬤ – 3 = 2

8 – ⬡ = 4   6 – ⬢ = 3   7 – ◻ = 5

▭ – 6 = 3   ⬭ – 5 = 4   10 – ✦ = 6

Draw a line to join each pair of stars with the
same answer.

4 – 3   8 – 5   9 – 7

10 – 3   9 – 2

7 – 4   6 – 4   7 – 6

Answers

Pages 4–5

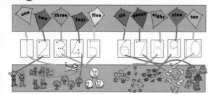

Page 6

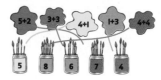

Page 7

There is more than one possible answer. Parents need to check their child's answers for this page.

Pages 8–9

6 biscuits altogether, 6 cakes altogether, 5 pizzas altogether, 7 ice creams altogether, 9 sweets altogether.
3 and 2 make 5 altogether, 4 and 3 make 7 altogether, 6 and 2 make 8 altogether.

Page 10

5 take away 2 leaves 3, 6 take away 2 leaves 4, 8 take away 2 leaves 6, 4 take away 2 leaves 2, 9 take away 3 leaves 6.

Page 11

5 children, 4 chairs, difference = 1.
7 children, 5 chairs, difference = 2.
6 children, 3 chairs, difference = 3.

Pages 12–13

4 sweets add 2 sweets = 6 sweets;
6 sweets add 1 sweet = 7 sweets;
5 sweets add 3 sweets = 8 sweets;
7 sweets add 2 sweets = 9 sweets.
6 drinks take away 1 drink = 5 drinks;
5 drinks take away 3 drinks = 2 drinks;
3 drinks take away 2 drinks = 1 drink;
7 drinks take away 4 drinks = 3 drinks.

Page 14

6 biscuits altogether, 6 cakes altogether. 6 and 2 make 8 altogether. 8 take away 2 leaves 6, 4 take away 2 leaves 2.

Page 15

line 1: 2 rabbits are hidden,
line 2: 1 rabbit is hidden,
line 3: 4 rabbits are hidden,
line 4: 5 rabbits are hidden.

Pages 16–17

2 + 3 = 5, 3 + 4 = 7, 4 + 5 = 9.
3 + 5 = 8 altogether, 4 + 2 = 6 altogether. 3 + 2 = 5, 2 + 2 = 4, 4 + 3 = 7, 5 + 1 = 6, 6 + 3 = 9, 4 + 5 = 9.

Pages 18–19

7 – 2 = 5, 5 – 2 = 3, 8 – 2 = 6.
Parents need to check child's answer for the last sum on page 18.
5 balls take away 3 balls = 2 balls,
4 balls take away 2 balls = 2 balls,
8 balls take away 4 balls = 4 balls.

Pages 20–21

4 + 2 = 6, 5 + 3 = 8, 7 + 2 = 9,
3 + 4 = 7, 6 + 4 = 10, 2 + 3 = 5.
5 + 2 = 7, 4 + 1 = 5, 3 + 3 = 6,
6 + 3 = 9, 3 + 1 = 4.
The missing numbers are:
blue rocket – 6, 9, 10; green rocket – 1, 3, 4, 8; red rocket – 8, 9, 12, 15.

Pages 22–23

6 – 3 = 3, 5 – 2 = 3, 8 – 4 = 4,
9 – 3 = 6, 10 – 2 = 8, 7 – 6 = 1.

Pages 24–25

6: 0 + 6, 1+ 5, 2 + 4. 8: 1 + 7, 2 + 6, 3 + 5. 9: 1 + 8, 2 + 7, 3 + 6.
7: 0 + 7, 1 + 6, 2 + 5.

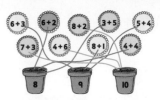

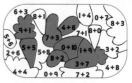

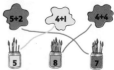

A rabbit and a carrot are hidden among the shapes.

Page 26

3: 4 – 1, 7 – 4, 3 – 0, 9 – 6, 8 – 5.
4: 7 – 3, 5 – 1, 9 – 5, 8 – 4, 6 – 2.
Possible answers are: 6 – 1, 8 – 3, 9 – 4.

Page 27

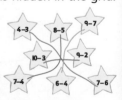

5 balls take away 3 balls = 2 balls,
4 balls take away 3 balls = 1 ball.

Pages 28–29

4 + 3 = 7, 6 + 2 = 8, 5 + 5 = 10, 9 + 1 = 10, 7 + 2 = 9, 3 + 5 = 8, 2 + 4 = 6, 4 + 4 = 8, 6 + 3 = 9. The missing numbers are: row 1 – 6, 8. row 2 – 10, 9, 8, 10. 4 + 3 = 7, 3 + 2 = 5, 4 + 5 = 9, 6 + 3 = 9, 2 + 8 = 10, 5 + 3 = 8, 6 + 2 = 8, 3 + 3 = 6, 3 + 7 = 10. The missing totals are: train 1 – 6, 9; train 2 – 3, 6, 8; train 3 – 3, 4, 7.

Pages 30–31

6 – 4 = 2, 7 – 3 = 4, 5 – 1 = 4,
8 – 5 = 3, 6 – 3 = 3, 9 – 4 = 5,
10 – 5 = 5, 7 – 4 = 3, 8 – 3 = 5.
The number 4 is hidden in the grid.

6–1	5–1	7–2	7–4	8–2	8–3
5–2	7–3	6–3	10–1	9–7	5–4
3–2	10–6	8–5	4–4	6–4	10–5
10–7	4–0	9–6	9–5	5–0	6–5
8–3	8–4	6–2	5–1	7–3	4–4
5–3	9–4	7–1	10–6	8–6	3–0

7 – 4 = 3, 6 – 2 = 4, 5 – 3 = 2,
8 – 4 = 4, 6 – 3 = 3, 7 – 2 = 5,
9 – 6 = 3, 9 – 5 = 4, 10 – 4 = 6.